My Granddad's a Bear

Written by
Jessica Watkins

Illustrated by
Marvin Alonso

A COLORING BOOK

Habershambooks

This Book Belongs To:

Today is a special day, the day my granddad is coming to town.

There was nothing that made us happier than spending time together.

Mom and I sat on the sofa after breakfast and waved goodbye as Dad left for work.

The airport is one of my favorite places to visit.

A big hairy person picked me up, and gave me the biggest hug; it was my granddad.

My mom must have picked up the wrong one because he was a bear, for sure.

My granddad went into the living room to nap.

My mom went into the kitchen to make lunch.

"How about we go and wake up your granddad for lunch." Mom said.

Looking at each other they burst into laughter.

"Mom, I got him.
I trapped the bear.

My mom came over, holding a huge purple box.

My granddad pulled out a picture of him holding me as a baby.

It wasn't so bad having a bear for a granddad.

Printed by Libri Plureos GmbH in Hamburg, Germany